MEDICINE-WATER

Mashkiq'Kiu-Ne'Pish
Kitch-Iti-Ki-Pi the "Big Spring"

MENOMINEE and CHIPPEWAY INDIAN
LEGENDS and MYTHS

By

INAQTIK ATANOQKEN
(Raven Legenbard)

JOHAN G. R. BANER
Ironwood, Michigan

JOHN I. BELLAIRE
Manistique, Michigan

FIRST EDITION

Printed in the United States of America

INAQ'TEK ATANOQ'KEN HOLITOPA IMMIYUKPALI

Meaning "the wise raven, that sings legends and myths; priest and lord of Yukpali." First title-name given by the Arapaho-Menomini prophet, Mianisee, second by Sachem Ekuskini.

Johan G. R. Baner, Ironwood, Mich.

ONA'WAY—OK'SHA

Meaning "physically awake, mentally alert." First name-title Chippewa, second name Choctaw, and given by Sachem Ekuskini.

John I. Bellaire, Manistique, Mich.

CONTENTS

Ona'way-Ok'sha.

INTRODUCTION

Kitch-iti-ki-pi has—brain, heart—soul! Hundreds of "many-wise" and "much-knowing" old Indians of dozens of tribes have said so, and mendacity is despised by mental titans.

They have delineated their oracular "star-mirror" Kitch-iti-ki-pi as I, a phrenoligist, built my craniological delineations; and, advised to do so by my comrade and ne'at, my collaborateur Ona'way-Ok'sha, I, or, rather, we, have herein followed the great example.

Thus:

The springs physical, mental and spiritual sources of manifestations are uttered in different "chapters" of this our work.

Ergo:

If you, the peruser of these pages, find your philosophical brain organs, Causality—Comparison enthroned in your Cerebrum, in that case you will see—depths herein, and abstruse mystic gold at their bottoms. So, if your reading mood is dictated by Intuitiveness, the brain-well of foreboding; in that case you will, I hope, find Kitch-iti-ki-pi's ocult wonders reflected in some of our descriptions. Your organ of Sublimity finds magnificence—yes, bardic grandeur in the spring itself, and I hope that we have projected some of it to your films. Lyricism will be detected by your Ideality, if that leads you, when reading our cantos. Even such moods as those uttered by Philoprogenitiveness, by Parental Love, will find their alter.

Different brains like different things.

If the brain organs Causality—Comparison rule its comrades in the Cerebrum, then only cold reason is judging the things seen and heard.

To satisfy such—I have written:

"THE DOUBLE SOUL OF KITCH-ITI-KI-PI."

Such people like, as a rule philosophy, with just a grain of humor as salt to it. I have given it in this Indian story.

Some love poetical Ideality, are controlled by just that brain-organ.

"INDIAN FRIENDSHIP" is a religious-moral story. It has touched all those who have read it.

All these purely Indian stories show DIFFERENT characteristics of the "Great Spring."

Together they are temperamental, physiognomical and craniographical delineations of "The Star-cradling Spring," "The Water, in which the Moon quenches its thirst," Kitch-iti-ki-pi.

Study the sky-mirror, the spring. Then read this our delineation. Then tell us how close to the original our copy, this work, has come.

Please!

They should be closely related. IF ELBERT HUBBARD was right, when giving one of us the title "word-wizard." Chas. S. Osborn, when naming him "Avatar." Stillman H. Bingham when bestowing this wreath on him: "You have an imagination or fancy that is almost riotous in its luxuriance, a vocabulary that amazes me with its resources, a grasp of metrical feats that is bewildering, and a sense of harmony that is admirable."

Inaqtek Atanoqken.

A Prophesy in regard to genuine Indian lore, myths, etc.

Alas, nearly all the old, lore-wise Inaqtek Atanoqkens, raven-wise saga-bards are gone. And, with them, the lore-myths, which I call myth-lores, because more of their substance comes from Atanken, myth, than Atanoqken Legend, his bardic son has supplied.

I, "The White Inaqtek Atanoqken," so called, who, perhaps, would have won the wished for "title-name" Kakakee Atanken, prophetic myth-bard, IF any of the real Red-bards had remained among us on Earth long enough— I alone am now retaining some few Indian myth-lores in my-memory. I never wrote them down, when they were told to me, or rather, hinted at, by my greatest great Sagabard, Mianisee. And other smaller such.

"Hinted at?" My tellers of myth-lores gave me just the—gems. I myself have had to create all of the frame-works.

A time will come, when open-work "novels," front—and backyard "dramas" of everyday life will be dethroned. Deeper readers will appear, and—Myth-Lore, Indian such and Nordic—no other,—regain their high-bench.

This, and most of my many, for those readers.

Inaqtek Atanoqken.

Kitch-Iti-Ki-Pi's Many Names

1—Kitch-iti-ki-pi. Kitchitaking—The Great Water. The Great Ones Water.

2—Kitchitakibing   —The Great Cool Water.

3—Ke'shinamin   —The Blue Sky I see.

4—Ki'shiwa-tshiwan   —The roaring, bubbling spring.

5—Tshiwa'set   —Sound of thunder.

6—Tawaq'ian'-nipeu   —Drum water.

7—Naq'ka'anaq'wigiwam   —Our home's evening star.

8—Niwa'wack'abog   —The Bubbling spring.

9—Wigiwame baq'ka-anaq —Menominee for "Our home's evening star."

10—Hu'to'to   —meaning "Thunderer" in the Omaha tongue.

11—Mashkiq'kiu-ne'pish   —Medicine water.

12—Noqko'ma's asha'kan
13—Noqko'ma's aqka   —Mother Earth's martar and her kettle.

14—Nima'nita-Ogemaqkua —Brain Queen.

15—Mita'Ogemaqkua   —Heart Queen.

16—Nip'u-Kisha   —Water of the Great One and "Great Water."

17—Kitch-iti-ki-pi   —is Ojibway for "I LOVE YOU."

18—Gitchee Mee-Goo-Sec-Nipe'u —"The Great Eagle's Water."

19—Ina'Maqki, Wok-Nipe'u   —"The Thunderbird's Water."

20—Kitch-Mokiton   —The great bubbling water coming or springing from the earth.

The new Michigan State Buildings at the entrance to Kitch-iti-ki-pi, the Palms-Book State Park, Manistique, Michigan

Flowers, Plants, Trees and Shrubs, Etc., at Kitch-iti-ki-pi Spring

Common Name	Latin Name
Prince's Pine	—Pipsissewa., Chimaphila Umbellata.
Dandelion	—Taraxacum, (Den Leonis.)
Trailing Arbutus	—May-Flower. Epigaea Repens.
Golden Rod	—Solidago Ulmifolia.
Butter Cup	—Ranunsulus Aeris.
Indian Turnip	—Arisaema Triphllum.
Fly Honeysuckle	—Lonicera Ciliata.
Marsh Hedge-nettle	—Stachys Palustris.
Blue Flag	—Iris Versicolor.
Canada Mint	—Mentha Canadensis.
Winter-green	—Pyrola Secunda.
Painted Trillium	—Trillium Erythrocarpum.
Spotted Touch-me-not	—Impatiens Biflora.
Evening Primrose	—Oenothera Niennis.
Wild Rose	—Rose Blanda.
Blue Violets	—Viola Obliqua.
Turtle-head	—Chelone Glabra.
Arrow-head	—Sagittaria Latifolia.
Wild Lily-of-the-valley	—Unifolium (Smilacina.)
Bunch Berry	—Cornus Canadensis
Twisted Stalk	—Streptopus Roseus
Golden Thread	—Coptis Trifilia.
Indian Pipe	—Corpse Plant Monotripa Uniflora.
False Solomon's Seal	—Vagnera (Smilacina) Racemosa.
Round Leaf	—Sun-dew, Drosera Rotundifolia.
Dog's Tooth Violet	—Erythronium Americanum.
Yellow Violet	—Ciola Pubescens.
Common Milkweed	—Asclepias Syriaca.
Star Flower	—Trientalis Americana
Squirrel Corn	—Dicentra Canadensis.
Duck-weed	—Sperodela Bolyrhiza.
Thicket Horsetail	—Equisetum pratense Ehrh.
Common Scouring-rush	—Equiseum Hyemale.
Fir Club-moss	—Lycopodium Selago.
Shining Club-moss	—Lycopodium Lucidulum.
Marsh-Marigold	—Caltha Palustris (Cow-slip).
Ferns Common Polypody	—Polypodium Vulgare.
Ferns Bracken	—Pteris Aquilina.
Fern Maiden-hair	—Adiantum Pedatum.
Fern, Sensitive	—Onoclea Sessibilis.
Sweet Vernal Grass	—Anthoxanthum Odoratum, (Sweet Grass.)
Hazel-nut	—Corylus Americana.
Wild Elder	—Aralia Hispida.
Marsh Everlasting Pea	—Lathyrus Palustris.

TREES

Balsam	—Abies Balsamea.
White Spruce	—Picea Canadensis.
Tamarack	—Larix Laricina.
White Pine	—Pinus Strobus.
Hemlock	—Tsuga Canadensis.
White Cedar	—Thuja Occidentalis (Arbor Vitae.)
Blue Beech. Water Beech	—Carpinus Caroliniana.
American White Beech	—Betula Populofiniana.
Yellow Birch. Gray Birch	—Betula Lutea.
American Beech	—Fagus Americana.
Elm	—Ulmus Americana.
Soft or White Maple	—Acer Saccharinum.
Sugar or Rock Maple	—Acer Saccharum.
White Ash	—Fraxinus Americana.
Black Ash	—Fraxinus Nigra.
Popular	—Populus Alba.
Ground Pine	—Lycopodium Obscurum.
Willow, Willow Bank	—Salix Luviarilis.
Wild Red Cherry	—Prunus Pennsylvanica.
Pin or Pigeon Cherry	—Prunus Pennsylvanica.
Choke Cherries	—Prunus Serotina.. Ona'way-Ok'sha.

Nearly all of the above mentioned plants and trees have been and are used by all our tribes; some for medicinal purpose, others as food, or for basketry, dyeing, weaving, pottery decoration, toilet, ceremonial uses, etc.

Let us inspect the ethnobotany of one of our most remarkable tribes, the Zuni Indians of the extreme western part of New Mexico, a tribe that, judging from its widely spread botanical nomenclature, may have originated it.

(Names in Latin and Zuni, the later is explained in English): also, in some cases, our own "every day names.")

Medicinal: sure that Ne'at Onaway forgot to mention some of the plants that grow near the "Big Spring," when he prepared the above list, I will add a few extras):

Artimisia frigida Carduaceam wild wormwood; Zuni name: To'-shoeha'chikia, meaning "seeds sweet leaf" (the gray wormwood, wrightii, is Halo kia'we, "ant seeds".) The former is made into a tea, which, if drank hot, is a remedy for colds (the last named has its seed sprinkled over burning coal—always by one of the Ant fraternity, the patient standing nude astride the coal-pot and thereby relieving his or her pain.)

Berula erecta, Water parsnip, Zuni: Pi'tkiaia, meaning, "Spring plant." Found near springs, and constitute part in a very potent medicine, known to only the highest medicine men.

Chenopodium Cornatum, Goosefoot, Zuni: Ha'techi, "Strong odor." Steeped in hot water, vapor inhaled to relieve headache.

Datura-metaloides D. C. Jamestown Weed, Zuni: A'neglakya, meaning, mystic boy." A narcotic, prepared and handled by the priests only. Our dangerous Thornapple, and noticed by myself in a field near Manistique, Michigan. Parent weed of the wonderfully beautiful Datura Cournocopia Arborea ("Angel's trumpet").

Eriogonum alatum, Buckwheat family. Zuni: {'shi'pa, meaning "slightly ill smelling." Root dried and pulverized; the powders preserved in "Love-bags" and sniffed to drive away miserable feelings.

Helianthus annuus L., sunflower. Zuni: O'matsapa, meaning "on tip of stem." Used, together with other ingredients, to cure rattlesnake bites.

New Mexico's flora is, of course, differentiating from that of Michigan, but Arrowheads both of them have, and one as interesting as the other. A myth tells that "Wios'kasi, the good one, shot them against Pteatee'mara, the grinner, who tried to spit in Kitch-iti-ki-pi's face, and thereby "make love dirty."

Kitch-iti-ki-pi's Coptis trifolia ("Gold-thread") grows also in Norway, Siberia, Kamtchatka, etc. Its medicinal uses are all known; bitter, and prepared as ordinary mouth wash. It also yields a beautiful yellow dye.

The Cornus Canadensis (Bunch Berry), mentioned in Onaway's list above, is closely related to Cornus cicinata, and may have the same powers, which are: Substituting Peruvian bark in intermittent fevers. C. florida and C. sericea, sisters of Canadensis whitens teeth, if the stripped branches are rubbed against them. C. officinalis, another relative, gives a scarlet color.

Dicentra Canadensis may, perhaps, be used for expelling worms from the human system. D. Cucularia does just that. Better not try it without advice from Indian medicinemen, or your own doctor.

"Dog's teeth" (Erythronium) I—let alone, since an old Indian told me that "it is good, but may bite, if wrongly treated." All I know about it is that "it should be mixed with something else, when used."

Lathyrus (everlasting pea) has—sixty known species, some used for that sickness, others for something different. L. tuberosus is food plant, but L. apaca's seeds is "good, when green, narcotic, when ripe."

Of Trailing Arbutus, Painted Trilliums, Lily-of-the-valley, and many of the rest on Onaway's list, I will say: Let them alone, if you have—heart and brain. They are—stanzas in Kitch-iti-ki-pi's wonderful poem, souls of the springs many spirits. Do not destroy them by picking. The wonder spring may be willing to give you one bloom of each as mementos. But hurt not the plant, when picking your gifts.

And now Kitch-iti-ki-pi's guardians, the trees. First of all remember that they, like the springs herbs and flowers, are inhabited by—spirits. Wisdom dwells in cedars, love in birches, power in oaks. The rowan tree, when standing close to a balsam or spruce tree asks questions and tells stories from and to those its friends. Raven and Crow are listening, and in that manner the sagas of Past are brought to the old and wise among the Red people. Raven brings them myths and legends, The crow told Montezuma that he should be on his guard against the Spaniards, "the devils," as Crow called them; had the emperor followed that warning, then he would have lived and ruled longer. Crow, the bird of foresight, prophesy, knew and knows because he hearkens to and understands what rowan, balsam and spruce whisper to each other.

All trees are givers. Givers of both physical and spiritual gifts. Red people make tepees and wigwams of their bark. Ne'paqaqkisag and a'kemaq'-tik, the black ash and the black elm gave bows to the Red man's fathers. And Aska, the pine "gave them many things and much." The birch—ah, if you gave your loved one a drop of birch-honey in a birch bark, dipped in Kitch-iti-ki-pi's water, then you know. Place a small peace of the bark from an eastward growing root of mo'nipiona'we, a tamarack in your asha'kan, in your mortar. Touch it with your asha'kanaq'tik, your mortar stick. Then feel in your pocket. GOLD. Of course, that must be done at exact midnight.

Stammering ends, if you hold the fruit of o'kapu'owe in your mouth, when talking. O'kapu'owe is hazel, as you may know.

And is not Sheshikima a ne'at, a superfriend to all the knowing ones. You—white people, call her Sugar-maple, and sweet she is. She gives you kwopo, baqwa-tenekan and shaka'shita, which means sirup, sirup-bread and wax-candy. Wax-candy—can you make that? Just boiling maple syrup, placed on snow and garbed in birch-bark. If for your loved one, then the bark should be dipped in the lovers' spring, Kitch-iti-ki-pi, and then dried by west sun.

Wotap, the fir-tree "talks to Wios'kasit, the ever good one, explaining your troubles to him, and bringing his promises back to you.

Hark! Do you hear birds, flowers, trees sing: "Kitch-iti-ki-pi"?

Did you hear the spring answer: "Kitch-iti-ki-pi"?

"I love—you."

"I love—you."

Inaqtik Atanoqken.

Birds-eye view of Kitch-iti-ki-pi the "Big Spring," 400 feet wide, 200 feet long and wide swift running stream running to Indian Lake

"Hawe Ini Kitchitikipi Tano'ka Noqko'ma Nime'nekem Bama'desewi."

It is in KITCH-ITI-KI-PI where mother Earth gives me (us) life, health.

One of Kitch-iti-ki-pi's many names is Mashkiq'kiu-e'pish, Medicine water. Some one, it may have been my ever wandering old friend the Arapaho bard and prophet Mianisee, the Wise Owl, or the older Headflyer of Flambeau, Wisconsin, told me this Menomini Indian tale decades ago. Later I heard it from the lips of a charming Menomini girl at Lost lake (also called Lake Baner, because of my building the settlement around it.) Vilas, County, Wis. Both times in the Menomini version and tongue. Depending on my memory I never wrote it down, wherefore parts of it is forgotten.

Kawatukan, principle of love in Hawatuk, the trinity, met and pitied Noqko'ma, our mother Earth.

Long before long ago, this happened.

Noqko'ma, at that time, had no flowery garments, not even the emerald shawl, which summer's fay, Nepenua, now hangs over her shoulders. Frost-weaving Kunikatan, now called Queen of Winter-world had given her neither frontlets, rings or other rime creations. And that queen had never thought of wrapping her soft snow ermine around the nude and charm-hungry Noqko'ma. Takwakwoa, Autumn's generous colormaid, had not thought of the hundreds of tints, which Kawatukan, God-mother of everything adorable, had given her, at Taqwakwoas, at the autumn queen's birth, the ever recurrant.

So the love maid, Kawatukan found Noqko'ma, found mother Earth in tears, crying because . . . well, her spirit knew Akamia's loveliness, heaven's loveliness. That spirit had been above the blue, and it remembered its bygone, dreamed of its future—there.

Kawatukan's both tears and smiles create. One her tear mingled with one of Noqko'ma's tears, and Noqko'ma became the owner of the jewels, all the gems, which we know mother Earth to possess in nowtime. Kawatukan smiled, and Noqko'ma had Sayikwakin's, Nepenua's Takwakwoa's and Kunikatan's —Spring's Summer's, Autumn's and Winter's garments in her wardrobe.

Then—Noqko'ma, then mother Earth smiled, also.

And she smiled again, when the heart maid Kawatukan had whispered something into her ears of the summer queen Nepenua, and the last named gave her lavender, mignonette, lily, rose and other fragrant herbs and blooms for Scentrealm.

Kawatukan is ALL-world's heart maid. So she could not remain with Noqko'ma always. Her tepee, woven from moon beams, lilac blooms and the virginal blue of Twilight's pinions—that her tepee is to be seen in all her realms at the same time, so Kawatukan is omnipresent, in the saddle of the thundergod's courser, Nanaboojoo's courser Hanaq'papeqtsi, the winged meteor, and in the grottos of Ana'maqki'ok, the underworld, realm of hopelessness, fear and their clan folks—omnipresent. Present with mother Earth, with Noqko'ma, too, always, though oft unseen. Noqko'ma did no longer see heaven's heart maid, became lonely, and—again she sighed, again she cried.

And again Kawatukan revealed herself.

That time mother Earth, Noqko'ma wanted "living and moving things, such as Akamia, heaven is filled with."

So she moaned.

Kawatukan alone is fully able to create anything for the worlds of Feeling and Fancy, so she tried to satisfy Noqko'ma's wishes. Had Noqko'ma known what she wanted, then, perhaps, Kawatukan could have copied her thought picture, which she now found confusing.

So she called: thus: "Kisha, brainy righteousness, Noqko'ma needs you!" "Kashe, willing power, Noqko'ma needs you."

And there and then Heart, Brain and Power, Kawatukan, Kisha and Kashe became Hawatuk, the trinity.

Noqko'ma, mother Earth, is thousand eyed and one eyed at the same time. The trinity placed itself so that it could read that single eye, the deepest, clearest of her many, the eye that reflects Kawatukan's own. The one of Noqko'ma's that, like Kawatukan's, whispers: "I LOVE YOU, KITCH-ITI-KI-PI" to everything.

Yes, in Noqko'ma's KITCHITIKIPI, in mother Earth's spring—the trinity tried to read her wishes.

But Noqko'ma's memory of "Heaven's living and moving things" must have been befuddled, and the results of the reading in her eye did not satisfy mother earth.

First Kawatukan and Kisha saw or thought they saw a bear pictured in Noqko'ma's KITCHITIKIPI. Both uttered the Menomini name of bear, and Owasse was produced by Kashe, by the third person in Hawatuk, the trinity, Power.

Noqko'ma inspected the beast, but shook her head, that was not what she wanted.

So the trinity tried again. This time it saw a bird in Kitchitikipi, and Kisha and Kawatukan mentioned "Inaqtek." Immediately a raven flew out of Kashe's, of Power's hands.

But Noqko'ma shook her head.

The result of the trinity's third trial became a Piwat'inot, a beaver, but Noqko'ma remained unsatisfied.

Now, bear means power, beaver means willingness to work and raven means thought and mental flight. The trinity combined them, adding hundreds of other qualities to their work, split the sum total of the whole and there stood Naqko'ma's satisfaction, Ina'niu and Mita'mu, man and woman.

KITCH-ITI-KI-PI has been called "Noqko-ma's asha'kan" and "Noqko'ma's akae, mother Earth's mortar and her kettle."

It is both, you ever questioning white Inaqtek Atanoqken, white Raven Sagabard.

Became that thus:

The trinity's gift to Noqko'ma, Ina'niu and Mita'mu, man and woman had offsprings in millions. And as few among them listened not to and followed not the warnings of their wise ones, so sickness came among them. Nepua, the transformer, made tshipais of men and women, ghosts of tribe folks.

It is true that mother Earth, Noqko'ma, always insisted on the return to her of all her gifts, so the me'io, the body parts of both Ina'niu and Mita'mu, man and woman were only loaned as coverings of the soul-sparks in them, loaned to the trinity, who in those earthen wigwams developed soul-sparks into soul-pyres, which, in due time were to become perfected wakondas, noble spirits in the trinity's home world Blueregion. But sickness squandered mother Earth's loan gifts, that or poisoned them. Often, also, a bantling's soul tepee was returned to her, to mother Earth as such, that is, without growing into a soul wigwam, developing into a man's or a woman's soul candlelabrum.

Kawatukan, the universal heart maid has many mirrors, but one of her clearest is—Kitch-iti-ki-pi. One morning, many parts of an aeon ago that was, one morning Kawatukan found her mirror Kitch-iti-ki-pi beclouded, wished herself down to it and—was there. Her wish is her pasikugary, her lightning-winged bearer twixt zone and zone. She found her mirror, mother Earth's eye, veiled in despair's gray wadmal, and asking Noqko'ma for a reason, she found that to be sickness in her tribes.

Kawatukan thought, but the maid of love is more heart, than brain, so she had to call upon the first principle of trinity, the wise and, when all the thought products are assembled in his cranium, alwise Kisha. She just wished him to Kitch-iti-ki-pi, and her wish brought him there in less time than none.

Together they too, heart and brain, made Noqko'ma's mirroring eye, Kitch-iti-ki-pi into a kettle-mortar, where-in Noqko'ma's own herbs could be pounded and cooked, become medicine for all her tribes.

Yes, brain and heart of the trinity. Hawatuk asked Ne'paqaqkwag'tik, the black ash to give that mortar-kettle part of its endurance, Ne'pakaku'aqtik, the black oak was to throw in fragments of its strength, Wigi, birch was called upon to offer drops of its sweetness.

Sheshikima, the maple, gave both bakwa'tene'kan and kwopo, both sugar and mead. All trees just gave, and freely. And those two parts of the trinity, Kisha and Kawatukan, also begged (they never command?) health-giving elements from cedar, spruce, poplars—from every tree and shrub that was —part of Kitch-iti-ki-pi's eyebrows.

Mianisee—not Headflyer, the Arapaho—not the Chippewa must have told me this story. Headflyer knew not the Suni Indian language, had never been in New Mexico. And my notes from olden time, when I, the compiler of this myth-tradition, spent twenty nights with Mianisee, then in tepee on the edge of Lake Buckataban, Vilas county, Wisconsin. My old notes on this subject show that my story teller used Suni names on the herbs, which he said had been placed in the mortar-kettle Kitch-iti-ki-pi, to be pounded and cooked therein, made into "all-healing medicine." Here I give a part of his, my story tellers, list of herbs, give his names, the explanations of those names, and their latin equivalents:

Ha' tsenawe, cold leaf, Achillea lanulosa, which makes Kitchitikipi's water "cold-healing."

Kwi-minne lokiana, gray root, Aster hesperius, "the sore-healing one."

Ke'nawe, salt weed, Astriplex canescens, "ant bite healer."

Ha'techi, strong odor leaf, Chenopodium cornatum, "head-ache healer."

Tu'ma ikiapokia, put into eye leaf, Crassina grandiflora, "fever and eye healer."

My name lists, containing about sixty plant names, is too long for my story, my repetition of Mianisee's (?) tradition.

Sufficient for my purpose when I repeat my saga teller's climax thus:

"Kawatukan and Kisha, Heart and Brain of our trinity, made an all healer out of the multi-named "Big Spring," Kitch-iti-ki-pi.

And all tribes knew it as such through long times and longer."

From some one, now forgotten, I have this in my notes:

"Parents used to seek names for their newborn in Kitch-iti-ki-pi: even the faraway Pomeroon Arawaks did so, and here a few of the names, which the spring is said to have "written in moss-runes or given in purls":

Satu, darling; Kakushika, big-eye; Sato-bara, pretty hair; Natukoro, lovely flower; We-shi, little fish.

Many, many are the myths, legends and allegories, which the sagabards of past generations have spun from Kitch-iti-ki-pi's rich materials. I know scores of them, "the old—old ones" know more. But the unprinted dozens will leave Redworld—with us.

O'mot and Mima'nita

From the all-Indian saga (or myth?) cycle "Pawakikanaq-tek"

"O'mot and Mima'nita," which means Stomach and Brain, is just a chapter from the probably all-Indian saga (or myth?) cycle "Pawakikanaq-tek," the mortar-pestel, a seemingly endless tale about—everything, deeply mythical in some of its links, subtly satirical in other components, resembling "Gulliver's travels." Some of its parts could be called "munchhausiads," or be linked into the lumbercamp lore of Paul Bunyan.

At least three stories in Pawakikanaqtik hints to Kitch-iti-ki-pi, but this one names the spring.

"O'mot lived on one side of Kitch-iti-ki-pi, Mima'nita lived on the other side of it. The former had nothing but an ever hungry stomach and an ever thirsty throat, the latter had built everything, planted everything, which his kaleidoscopic brain had visualized. Birch had given him white bark and much bark, so his wigwam was large and beautiful. Beaver and Bear had supplied him with mattress and quilt. He had plenty to eat and drink, because he, unlike O'mot, eat to live—not the reverse.

O'mot was able to see Mima'nita's riches, and comparing them with his own lack thereof, he became jealous, just like some of our time's people, though, of course, not you or I. And hunger, thirst and jealousy together made him inclined to make himself the owner of Mima'nita's property which he thought easy enough, when he noticed the rich ones small size, and he saw his own enlarged by the magnifying water of Kitch-iti-ki-pi.

The spring was wider, but no deeper in those times. And then as now Kitch-iti-ki-pi seemed to be much more shallow than it is—about twenty, instead of sixty feet deep. So O'mot, being too lazy to walk around it for the attractions on its other side, tried to wade the expanse. All stomach people are giants, and O'mot was—tradition does not give his height, but tells that he was three men and a child tall, so it's easy for you, listener, to figure out, that the distance between his feet and his head might have been—just might! —about—just about! not much less than fifteen, not much more than twenty-five feet; if absolute accuracy is demanded, then guess twenty-one feet, five and a half inches.

Yes, O'mot tried, just tried to wade over and take possession of Mima'nita's comfort.

Food and drinks are comfort, you know; all of it—for stomach people. Brain folks insist on more than that, much more.

I, the white teller of this tale, I do not know just how to say "darn it!" in Chippewa, Menomini or other tribe tongues. But something equivalent to "darn it," perhaps with plus and double plus added, was what O'mot roared, when he had spouted, erupted—thrown up those hogsheads of water, which

Kitch-iti-ki-pi had poured into him during his trip to her down stairs, sixty feet below her attic-part.

He did not free himself from all that Kitch-iti-ki-pi had bestowed upon him, enough was retained to keep him baloonized and wet throated nearly a week, and during that time he had so much of physical remorse over the too liberal consumption and a cold, that he never even thought of Kitchiti-kipi's better side. Conscientious pangs, also, for having no room to offer the eatable beasts who seemed to know his condition.

A week or ten days later O'mot was a fully healed stomach again; cured, and of course, hungry. So his thoughts wandered back from castigation to mastication, words he had heard from Mima'nita, the brain man, who was tribal leader—priest, bard and medicine man and, therefore, and because of his wish to picture his thoughts, feelings, etc., correctly, had become a perambulating word mine.

Yes—excuse this sagabard for imitating his red ditto, adding byways to the highways of lore!—yes, O'mot tried his best to imitate Mima'nita; the latter's euphony became the former's . . . . hm, all of us have listened to both murmurs and thunders from empty and overfilled stomachs. Example: Mima'-nita's "caveat," take warning, because "cave in," when drummed by O'mot and the brainman's supplication to the universal Ego, which sounded "Facinate my soul by prophetic incantation," that became "Vaccinate my hole by phonetic stimulation," when Stomach moaned it.

The above may not be word for word what Brain said and Stomach repeated, but here something nearer verbatism::

"White people talk of food and drink always and everywhere. But they are falsely ashamed of the results of their consumptions, although knowing that —eliminations are much more important. I really fear that some of the white sagabard's listeners will say "ush," when he tells them these:

"Stomach was, of course, too idiotic to raft himself over to Brain's side of Kitchitikipi. Too idiotic, also, to walk around that water. His only way of getting there was, as he concluded, to—empty the spring by drinking it dry. And that he tried. He stood exactly where Crooked Brook now starts out for its journey toward the lake, and—well, that was the birth hour of Crooked Brook. You see Stomach could not hold all he took in of the spring's water, most of it must have an outlet, and . . . oh, yes, Crooked Brook and Indian Lake came into existence through O'mot's, stomach's efforts that time.

Poor, foolish Stomach, I, the red sagabard, who tells this to my white brother, you, I am sorry for him. How could he know that Sun and Brain (Keso and Mima'nita) were such friends that the former carried back to Kitch-itikipi all the water that had passed through O'mot. He, Stomach, had no knowledge of the fact that the under-earth beings, the anamaqkius cooled the so returned fluid in their Coldworld."

So he spake, the red sagabard to me, the white.

So and thus:

"Those that are older than our oldest, twice as old, they claim that Gitchi Gummee's water came from Kitchitikipi, through O'moth's efforts. But that lake—white ones call it Superior, that lake is many times big, and we young old people—I am but one hundred and seventeen some times—, we young old half doubt that, that wide and long and deep would have so clear water, if it had—had gone through Stomach's—hm, processes.

Maybe, though, Maybe.

I never call another man's "truth" my "lie," except when I am far away from ears; the lier may have had more food, then I have had."

No, O'mot did not empty our spring. And he did not disturb Brain.

A few days later than soon, he felled a pinetree right into the spring. This I know, because I have seen the tree. From O'mot's side that pine seemed to bridge the gape between Stomach and Brain. But it did not do so. Stomach was, of course, not intelligent enough to end his wandering at the end of the tree, and so it happened that Brain lassoed Stomach and pulled him up on his side, Brain's, with the help of the only nine elks that were near enough to hear his, Brain's command.

That was the very last time Brain asked elks for any help. Stomach did all the work, if he was hungry enough, thirsty enough.

When he was both, but still unwilling to work, then Brain told him to feed on the three-ended sausage, slake his thirst from the downside up spring or end his cravings with a rope around his central part.

That Stomach does but seldom."

Well, there you, reader, you listener have one of the chapters of Pawakikanaq-tik, which I for my part do not understand. The rest is nearly as understandable.

Inaqtik Atanoqken.

Dock and landing at Kiitch-iti-ki-pi the "Big Spring" with load of sightseers on raft viewing the springs boiling on the bottom.

The Double-Soul of Kitch-Iti-Ki-Pi

The sum total of a heart's, a brain's utterings, if in whispers or roars, jubilations or tears, hid or manifested, is—their soul, their complete mutual ego.

The amoeba has the power and the will to change, expand.

It goes forward, upward; becomes—man, which is embryon of—wakonda, spirit, and, ultimately, manido, goal.

The amoeba, the embryon, the man—are electrons, molecules, lobes in —the universal, ego.

Parts of Aba, Wakan, Hesananin, Hawatuk, god.

Ergo: soul—sparks in — everything.

We have heard of Kitchitikipi's Mita'tshiok, her shade of shadows." That is not Kitchitikipi's only soul-spark, but an aggregate of soul amoebae, a composite of everything from the animal, vegetable, and, even, mineral spheres, that have drank the springs elixirs and remained with it for—more.

Notice those moss-covered trees? They had soul-sparks of their own, and are retaining them as such.

But they bubble their dirges and dithyrambs in group.

They are Kitchitikipi's orchestra.

Instruments therein.

Voices.

Hark: That softly bleating tune comes from Omes'kos, from Elk. He drank this crystal, saw his own beauty reflected in it, adored it, and remained with what he considered his spouse. He sings lovesongs even now.

That drumming sound comes from Wabbos, Hare. The reflection of his own ears scared him and hypnotized him to remain.

That lovely soprano . . . hm . . I wonder, if I should tell you how that came to be included in Kitchitikipi's chorus? Will just hint at it. The owner of that voice was deeply in love with her tribe's bravest brave. He fell in battle, and Kitchitikipi's own soul-fay Kawatukan, the great mystery, kissed the heartbroken maid to slumber at her own breast.

Yes, Kawatukan, the heart fay, Nanaboojoo, the thunderer and Manabush, the teacher of the philosophy of experience—those three noble spirits developed Kitchitikipi's soul spark into what it now is.

Her own.

So she—Kitchitikipi is—tripple-gendered, seemingly, or, at least, two: masculine in magnificence, feminine in lyric beauty—so she has the peculiarities of the three: Kawatukan's tender heart—she always gives; Nanaboojoo's, the thunderer's majesty, and Manabush's, the super-man's wisdom.

She smiles in sunshine, frowns in clouds, like all her sex.

She is pining for gifts, like all her sisters; and she is apt to take what she wants, if it is not offered.

Red people fear her ill will, so they throw her gems, which they themselves yearn for—money for money, wisdom's cedar bark for wisdom, rowan blooms for hypnotic power, spotless birch-bark for dependable love, etc.

What do you want? Love. Try Kitchitikipi. Mumble her the name of your adored one, and throw a really spottless birchbark into her lap, bend your head toward the water queen, and . . . well, I tried it, bowed too deeply and Kitchitikipi took my watch and gave me—a cold.

She is still keeping the former.

A woman she is, Kitchitikipi.

You will procure "cold feet?," if you approach her minus respect.

Sure of that.

And she will win you, if she wants you.

Sure of that also.

She won me, is keeping me in her retinue of admirers, and only one other charmer has been able to win and hold this "boy."

She is Queen of hearts, so I gave her that "title-name" long ago: Mita-Ogemaqua, Heart-queen.

Nima'nita-Ogemaqkua also—brain-queen also.

Yes, the sum total of our inherited endowment, the unfolding thereof, together with that, which we derive from experience, universal such and our more individual—is soul. Surroundings add to it, subtract from it, but our ultimate ego is—soul.

The cedartree's sighing, the balsam's graveness are soul manifestations. The birch utters soul-glee, the willow utters soul-woe.

Everything is endowed with—soul, undeveloped such.

Every tree, shrub, flower, beast and bird near Kitchitikipi has given her soul molecules.

And received such from her in exchange. Kitchitikipi has a marvellous soul—essence.

Find it.

Indian Friendship

(The Ojibwa Indians call this tradition "Ki'tcimak'wa hini Nigig-wug," meaning Big-bear and Otter. With them the legend starts and ends at Niwa'wacke'abog, the bubbling spring KITCHITIKIPI, near which the one-sided friendship is born and dies. The Menomini Indians' lore-chapter "Seko hini Owassee," Weasle and Bear tells the same tradition in the same form, but calls Kitchitikipi "Nipe'u-Kisha," which means both "Water of the Great one," and "Great Water." The last named rendition of the tale does not end at Seko's and Owasse's graves, but takes their spirits to, first Chipiapo's the ghost teacher's school realm in Miqkigan's Nipe'u, Lake Michigan, and, ultimately to the boundary line between Manitou-wauk, Spiritworld (not Manitowoc, great hunting ground!), the boundary line twixt that and "Mama'tshim-kesikoq-mihi'gan," the Indians, path of to-day. The deeper ending of the Menomini story makes me choose just that here.)

Seko and Owassee were born on the same day, under the same clan totem, but Seko on the south side, Owassee on the north side of Bubbling Spring, (Kitchitikipi).

Their cradle-bags had the same forms, were made out of related materials, but Owasse's hung so that its bantling never faced the bubbling spring and the warning sun at the same time.

The tree, from which the bag swung, grew on the north side of the spring.

Seko's cradle-tree grew on the south side of the bubbler, so he faced sun and spring always.

And in due time Owasse developed power, patience and true kind-heartedness.

And in due time Seko developed less of all those qualities, but more of . . . well, Seko means weasle.

Wako lived on the south side of Kitchitikipi in those times, and he became Seko's teacher.

Wako means—fox, red fox.

Both Owasse and Seko became swains in due time.

As boys they picked berries from forests, fields and swamps, but although Owasse picked most of their mutual pickings and carried most, still his parents found only few, and small in his basket. Seko had the many and the large.

Both of the youths loved Ota'qanimau, Charmmaid, who ridiculed the big and clumsy and grave Owasse, but smiled at Seko, the in dance light footed, in embrace flattering.

Ota'qanimau lived on Seko's side of the bubbling spring.

On Seko's side.

Where Seko's teacher Wako lived.

Owasse was invited to Seko's and Ota'qanimau's, Weasel's and Charm-maid's wedding feast, and his invitation-bark roared: "Bring all, you have!" by subtly whispering: 'Don't bring much.''

Owasse brought all, he had to the feast, so his friend and his friend's bride placed him just outside of the wigwam that Owasse had built for the pair out of birchbark, cut from Owasses only birchtree, and carried to Seko's side of the bubbling spring.

Later Owasse's spruce-bark hut, his tepee had to be enlarged, because Sheboygan, Hollow-bone, a wandering old woman of unknown tribe, became sick near it and won Owasse's sympathy. Sheboygan paid his benevolence by forcing him into marrying her and become stepfather to a whole clan of children.

Neither Seko, nor his wife came to Owasse's and Sheboygan's wedding feast, although invited without hints of bringing wedding gift.

Owasse, being a good hunter, brought much of his best meat to his friend's wigwam; and, although he and his had but simpler fish to their meals; Owasse exchanged brook-trout for mumbled "thanks."

Years past, and age arrived with sickness, sickness with death. For both Seko and Owasse. Just before the last named ended, he was heard to mumble thus: "I hope that Seko becomes well soon." And just before Seko ended, he said: "I hope that Seko becomes well soon."

Seko's grave was dug under a cedar and on the crown part of a hill from which both the bubbling spring and Daybreak's daughters could be seen. Seko's grave was lined with soft beaver skins, once belonging to Owasse.

Owasse's grave was unlined, and a little too close to the marshland. No totem tree shaded it. And the bubbling spring could not be seen from it. But glorious twilight, twinkling star and sun and moon beams found it.

They find all graves.

All.

Trush sang friendship's teary, but hopeful dirge over Owasse.

Chikako, skunk wished his "Remain there" over Seko's turfs.

Here the Chippewa tradition ends. But the Menomini's adds this:

Costly baqwatenekan and kwɔpɔ, maple sugar and maple wine in Seko's grave hut. That, but no mourners near it.

Corn bread in Owasses' hut, cornbread and always pure water from the bubbling spring. Tear eyed friends near it, wife, step children and more.

Bubbling spring, Kitchitikipi, near which Seko and Owasse were born, and where their graves were located, that spring is connected to Miqkigan, the wide water, by Waki'nin, crooked creek, through which spring and lake send messages to each other. Wakinin told Miqkigan about Seko's and Owasses' homelessness, and Miqkigan mumbled the news into the ears of

Chipiapos, the ghost-teacher, the one that developes ghosts into spirits pre-
pare them for Spiritworld, Manitou-wauk.

So he, Chipiapos sailed up to bubbling spring, to Kitchitikipi in his
strong and fast going canoe Ocpe'ta, the flyer, and during that trip the brook
whispered many words into the ears of the canoe, words that the canoe repeated to the ghost teacher, Chipiapos.

So that noble spirit, that wakonda knew much about Owasse's true, Seko's
untrue friendship, knew much about it before the bubbling spring, Kitchitikipi,
told him all.

Chipiapo's is as fair in his judgements, as Kisha Manido himself, the Great
Spirit himself. So he expects no more from a ghost, from a tshipai then a
reasonable development from spirit spark toward spirit flame. And although
he listened to and compared what the spring had bubbled to the creek, the
creek had purled to the canoe and the canoe had whispered into his, Chipiapo's
ears, yet he wanted to study Seko and Owasse in his own domain, Miqkigan.

And there he brought the two ghosts.

Miqkigan means both path and court; path leading to court also. It
has a roof of speaking water, reporting such. Water from thousand springs,
thousand brooks; all reporting to Chipiapos in the court, Miqkigan.

Ghost paths lead to spirit paths, lead to Miqkigan.

No, some of the former lead back to Redworld, for those to wander, who
are undeveloped, are given another chance in new bodies, become reincarnated,
as you white people name it.

Seko was near that condemnation. Chipiapos had placed all kinds of
comfort, food, and drinks near the two, and, as before, Owasse got the least
of it, Seko grabbed the best.

So, after four times three days, Seko was placed upon a path leading
back to Redworld for rebirth there. No moqkasines were given him and
nothing but hard corncobs were to be found in his lunch basket. Cicerone
was not needed, because that path is on the bottom of a deep ditch.

There Owasse saw him, saw him in tears for the first time.

Owasse saw his friend from his bloom covered seat in the canoe that
knows nothing about time or space, Joyworld's star spangled, blue.

Owasse sighed and cried because of Seko's terrible fate, and Chipiapos
could not wipe his cheeks dry. So he, the ghost teacher just had to find a space
for Seko in Owasse's canoe, after having figured out that the last named had
done three times more good during his life, than his talents called for. Seko's
record showed that his good deeds numbered not half of what the trinity had
expected from him. Together the two records more than balanced the trinity's
demands . . .

This story in full is to be found on pages 229-233 of my large Swedish volume "Barr." Here I must exclude parts of its lovely ending, and give just this:

"Akamia's manidos and wakondas, all the spirits of heaven wondered why a shining arrival and a drab one could land arm in arm on the shores of Bluerealm. But Chipiapos explained and begged, begged and explained, and begged, begged and explained, and so the starry portals opened for both Seko and Owasse, Weasle and Bear.

Mother of Winds

A Menomini legend, perhaps Na'motam himself, my very first Menominitic saga-teller "Tell-the-truth" (that is the meaning of his Indian name) himself—a legendarian told me this:

No'tenan, the wind maidens did not exist always. Far from always. Nothing existed always.

Everything was still and silent before they came.

No "baa" from the elk, no "wovv" from the dog, nor "rrr" from the bear, no haha" from the girl, no "I want it" from the swain.

The drum said nothing, and the forest slumbered, till the winds came, which was many days before yester-day.

Many, many days before.

Manabush, the foolish little Indian, who had gone to Blueworld, heaven, because he wanted to become less foolish, he had just returned to Earth again, so to make our mothers our fathers less foolish.

He had wings, when he came back, raven wings.

He landed not many days walk from the spirit makers' big water, Miqkigan.

Not many days walk from Chipiapo's, the spirit maker's Miqkigan, where he makes spirits out of ghosts.

And Manabush built himself a white wigwam near a spurting spring, a boiling spring, that moved its lips always, but said nothing, uttered no sounds.

That was long, long before yesterday.

The foolish little Indian Manabush was at that time the very wise Manido Manabush, Spirit Manabush; wiser than all Indians together.

But Blueworld, where he had been schooled, had song, had music, had sounds. And Manabush knew that heaven's no'tenans, heavens winds produced all of that.

It was evening, June evening. The moon and the stars shone down in the bubbling spring. Perhaps they mirrored themselves in it. Maybe they drank its clear, cool water. Manabush knew, but I don't know.

*Public Highway approaching Kitch-iti-ki-pi the "Big Spring" from the south
A most delightful shady drive.*

Bluerealm had tuned the man-manido's, Manabush's ears for sounds, and without them he felt his heart gray.

So he bent over the boiling spring's crystals and roared: "Spirits of the deep, sing me a song!"

He roared just so.

Roared.

And the first born daughter of the mother of winds, begotten through the voice of Manabush, was born.

She spoke and sang deeply, sonorously, but not in harmony with the color of Nepenua's mantle, not softly, like the tints in June's garments of twilight and moon beams.

Manabush admired that voice, but he did not adore it.

He named it "Atshi'kesiwa'enan," which means North wind now, but meant Cold wind, when the world was young.

Again he commanded, though not in roar, but—well, his command was given in a mixture of tunes, tremulous, alluring and imploring.

And the answering voice was an echo of his own.

Imploring, alluring, tremulous—tantalizing.

That voice he both adored and feared, and adored again.

Some times.

Manabush named it "Ashmuq'kaha-no'ten," which now means east winds, but at that time meant "everything mixed."

Then Manabush called the heart maid of Blueworld, and she came down to Bubbling Spring and him. He did not need to tell her his wishes, she knew his wants and called: "Mother of the wind-maids, send up Shawananon, the south wind to Manabush—kind wind mother, do."

And Shawananon came, sang and won.

Won Manabush's heart.

All hearts.

Three of the four wind sisters then sang from the bubbling water.

Three.

Till Kawatukan called the fourth.

Softly, yes, tenderly the goddess of love called: "As'nik Nowe'nan, West-wind, you flute maid of Twilight's orchestra, you metheglin, brewed by tune world's most tender beam fay, come."

Then all the wind maids sang, sometimes together, oft each one by herself.

Manabush could hear all the wind queens, but he saw none of them. He heard Northwind and Eastwind, and he also heard Southwind and Westwind. But see them, that he could not do. "Can you," he spoke thus to Kawatukan, heaven's queen of hearts, "can you tempt them into materialization, materialize them? If so, then please, do." And she granted his wish partly, she called forth wind mother's two youngest daughters, Southwind and Westwind. He, Manabush himself materialized Northwind and Eastwind, after he had seen and heard how Kawatukan produced and presented Westwind and Southwind.

Yes, there they stood, all the wind maids.

Northwind was then, what it remains today, gold locked, gray eyed, stately, yes, majestic. All that, but cold. Winter cold. Admirable, but, perhaps, a little manly. Not enough of woman, if compared with Southwind and Westwind. Proud, stern, overbearing, but, but admirable. She looked at Manabush, but gave him no smile; and Kawatukan's smiles, them she did not repay with smiles from her own beautiful but compressed lips.

Eastwind was shorter and fuller, than the oldest of the four; red headed also. That and brown eyed. And she smiled cynical smiles and tender such at, not only Manabush and Kawatukan, but at Bear and Wolf and Fox as well. She smiled at everything, frowned at everything, offered kisses to all and claws to all. Moody, changeable she was, fifty women in one woman, and none knew the other. She seemed to glory over her ability to attract and repulse, but some times Manabush thought himself see woe in her eyes, when she felt that—her kaleidoscopic nature turned her gains into losses.

Southwind's voice materialized into such a woman as most men instinctively try to win; she smiled at everything, like the goddess of love herself, like Kawatukan herself. But, Kawatukan's album has but one clear picture that of Nanaboojoo, the first born son of the combined trinity and the fairest of fair Indian maids, Nanaboojoo; The god of thunder, of lightning of rain, the one that none but the heart maid Kawatukan ever tamed, the one that roars blessings. Southwind, Shawananon smiled at all creation, just like Kawatukan. But her Nanaboojoo received her warmest smiles, her only kisses.

Southwind was and is rose cheeked, rose lipped. Born so, retained so. And she had not only a rightly formed frame, but warm and tender velvet thereon. As today.

"Westwind—oh, Westwind!"

So Manabush, so Kawatukan exclaimed, when that fay, when As'nik Nowe'nan appeared. Stepped out of that Bubbling Spring, that formerly mute spring, whose labology had been voiceless aeons of years and many more. Undescribable, irrestible, worthy of a god's veneration—such she was, the wind mother's youngest daughter, Westwind, As'nik Nowe'nan.

Was and—is.

The chain of Atanoqkens had many links between the first teller of this tradition and me, the one that now retells it to you. Each Atanoqken, each sagabard have seen—his own Westwind. I, Inaqtek Atanoqken, I Raven

Sagabard have met, adored, embraced and kissed mine—long, long ago. When my heart had summer's blood. An average lifetime ago. I saw her, bent the knees of my heart for her, embraced and kissed her a thousand times.

But describe her, deliniate her—that I can not.

Her name was, is and will ever remain Titatonga. And the euphony of her name was, is and will remain the euphony of its bearer.

Titatonga?

Rose of Heaven.

I have fancied her smiles in other wind maids, and have called the smiling mouths Titatonga.

I have fancied the pleasing, warming apple-bloom voice of Titatonga as coming from the throats of other wind maids.

But the original Titatonga, mine and that at the Bubbling Spring, was—one, and sincere and constant.

Undescribable.

So the mute daughters of Bubbling Spring, Northwind, Eastwind, South-wind and Westwind were given voices and called up from their mother's bosom. The first two named by Manabush, the man-god, the last two by Kawatukan, the heavenly fay of hearts.

There they stood, there they spoke, to each other and to Heartmaid and Mangod. There they sang, the queenly, but marble cold Northwind, the beau-tiful, but undependable Eastwind, the lovely Southwind and the adorable Westwind.

Atshi'kesiwa'anan in mantle of snow flakes and diadem bestowed upon her by Aurora Borealis, the queen of Northlight's glowing realm.

Asmuq'kaha'notan, clad in Dawning's many colored garments and Morn-ing's frontlet in her locks.

Shawana'non, wreated in the smile of loveliness, draped in veil of myrtle-green and rhododendron bloom. A constellation crowned her.

As'nish' Nowe'nan, beaming in afterglow's ermine and dew pearls, and with the eveningstar adorning her adorable self.

Four visions—realized. Manabush was satisfied, and so was the heart maid Kawatukan. He, the man god, "the in heaven to wise man educated earthly fool," became exhausted by admiration, adoration. And she was called back to her tepee of lilac, lilies-of-the-valley, forget-me-nots and pink-tinted, fragrant roses in the inner heaven, Akamia, where thoughts, feelings and fancies develop and materialize when uttered.

Manabush must have gone to sleep, in spite of the wind maids' song, dance and laughter, in spite of his wish to admire and adore the marble cold, the burning, the sunny and the chastest beam from the ever virtuous moon of spotless Taquakwoa, of Autumn.

Yes, Manabush had slept . . .

When he awoke, then he found a grinning, dwarfish witch by his side, the fun maker Nanapolo himself. Unwise people call him devil, but he is just personified humor, although one of his eyes has the gleam of satire. Trouble maker, that he was, is and shall remain, although oft against his own will.

Manabush laughed at the dwarf's jokes, at his contortions, his mimicry, his tail, which he always tried to hide, his short, horny head "ornaments," of which he seemed to be proud, and his ever winking ears. But Manabush did not laugh long, after Nanapolo had seen the four beautiful wind maids, and—fallen in love with them all.

Manabush considered Nanapolo's chances to win any one of them quite impossible, of course; but he found one of the maids—guess whom! smiling at the dwarf, yes, even stroking him over his protuberant "ornaments." Fearing that the discernment of the other three wind maids were as quick to lose their equilibrium, Manabush threw the cause of his fear, Nanapolo, into the Bubbling Spring, but only to find the hag of temptations, Aqki'nakoshi, "the terrible one," step out of it. And that witch, that strumpet became uncontrolable to both Manabush and the queen of heart, heaven's queen Kawatukan.

She "the terrible one," has tempted all four wind maids ever since.

Tempted and excused and bewildered.

No, not even Kawatukan could destroy Aqki,makoski, the terrible one; neither could Kisha.

But those two together called Anaq'enabaqtan out of the heart of the wind maids' mother, Bubbling Spring, and she whispered advise and warnings into ears, which had been poisoned by the terrible one's temptations.

Anaq'enabaqtan means Star-dream, and she is just that. She originated in Above and has often been called "Kawatukan's nightingale" and "Virgin-love."

But the terrible one is much taller, much wider, than Stardream, so she is able to reach the ears of even the tall Northwind.

Stardream is much shorter, much slimmer, so she finds it an arduous task to reach high enough, even when standing on her toes.

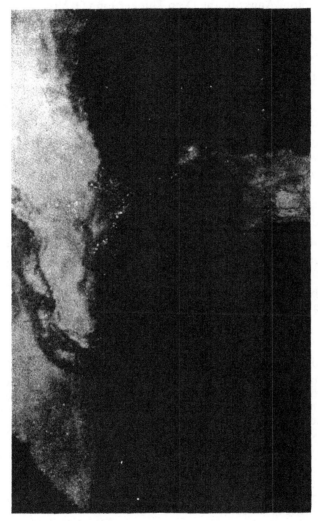

Craters boiling in bottom of Kitch-iti-ki-pi the "Big Spring" like volcanoes. These two craters go into full eruption about every two hours, throwing sand and sediment many feet into the body of the spring

What Nah-Ben-Ay-Ash Told to Hofobi Anukfili

So he spake, so Nah-ben-ay-ash, the Wind-driven-Cloud, the holy one—so he spake to Hofobi Anukfili, the Deep Thinker John O. Viking, Ishpeming, Mich. still among us, and still the great psycho-Indianologist.) Thus he spake:

"When long ago was thought of as the time far back of to-morrow, then a well shielded, well armed clan of the Menomini tribe took and held the holy water, Kesha's, Kashe's and Kawatukan's—Hawatuk's, the trinity's spring, KITCH-ITI-KI-PI.

Saying: "We, the clan—the ruling clan of Pakash'tshke'u, phratry, swift flying hawks," we need the waters of righteousness, power and love, the water of Kisha-Kashe-Kawatukan, Hawatuk's water, KITCH-ITI-KI-PI.

You and your mothers, you and your fathers drank it since your tribal domain was in a bantling's bag.

And you folks of the Chippeway tribe, you are now blessed with health and wealth.

We are not.

Our graves are many and small, yours few and large.

So we need it, take it, control it—the water of KITCHITIKIPI.

But we return it to you Chippewa's, when—pehike'wok—when two paddle (it)."

So our tribe Chippewa-Ojibwa lost KITCHITIKIPI.

For a long time and longer.

Hawatuk, the trinity did not interfere, so he may have found the change of ownership, imagined ownership, satisfactory.

Hawatuk knew that Kitchitikipi's real owner was—Hawatuk.

But he also knew that his Chippewa's needed water, good such. Therefore he pointed the fingers of righteousness, power and love, Kisha's Kashe's and Kawatukan's—therefore he pointed his three-fingered hand, Hawatuk's, the trinity's toward emptiness, thought the word "Nipeshe," lake, and Mama'tshim Nipeshe, Indian Lake, became Mama'tshim Nipeche.

I tell you this in the Menomini tongue, because I heard the tradition so uttered."

So Nah-ben-ay-ash spoke to Hofobi Anukfili, so wind-driven Cloud to deep Thinker, the Ojibwa-Menomini had that to tell his, then, young friend the Swedish-American Choctaw-Cheroki.

That and this:

"I do not know which widishi-anun—which phratry of the Chippewas' received the loan of Mama'tshim Pipeshe, Indian Lake from Hawatuk. My teller did not tell, and his teller of tales, his Atanoqken had not told.

But this:

"Matche-Hawaituk, the man-teasing bad one—not a devil, such we Indians had none before white people came among us—Matche-Hawaituk made the Chippewas hate the Menominis, the Menominis hate the Chippewas, so tomahaks were blooded and arrows smeared. The formers' Ogemah, their chief—chief would not exchange "Ho!" with the latters' Ogemah, and his daughter Anaq-Mick'isik, his daughter Star-eye was forbidden to look in the direction of Mama'tshim Nipeshe, the Indian Lake, where Prince Oshkosh the Bearclaw, son of Chippewa's Ogemah, had his wigwam standing.

Matche-Hawaituk is a trickster, a real tshi'sa'saqjua; some say that he is the father of them all. He is the origin of all mirages, those of hope and love and the rest. So he pictured the stately and handsome on Anaq-Nick'isek's sky, and copied her beauty and loveliness upon his own.

And thus he, Matche-Hawaituk, made the two fall in love with each other.

Then he bound them together with the crimping and stretching baqu'okta, the love belt, which all of us have felt, though only Kawatukan, the love maid have seen and, some times, smiled on it.

So Matche-Hawaituk ordered the belt to crimp, which it did, faster and faster, more and more, till Anaq-Mick'isik, the Ogemaqkua, the princess of the Menominis stood on her side of a roaring stream, which the love maid, Kawatukan herself had placed there; Prince Oshkosh, though a great swimmer, had to remain on the stream's other side for the time being.

But Matche-Hawaituk tried his belt again. And again. The hot Nepenua Keso, the summer sun drank the stream narrow and shallow in due time, and one evening Oshkosh found that he could touch Anaq-Mick'isik's finger points with those of his burning own. Next evening the two lovers clasped hands over that stream of—shyness, and when Tepeke'so of Takwakwoa, the moon of Autumn gave its domain silver garments, then the princess became so adorable, the prince so handsome, the belt so strong that breast met breast, lips met lips for the first time.

Their breasts. Their lips. Oshkosh's and Anaq-Mick'isik's.

Then?

O, they swam side by side in Mama'tshim Nipeshe, the Indian Lake. They drank KITCHITIKIPI'S elixir out of the same birch goblet, when moon and stars let them hide in the cloak of night.

Then?

Why, you know, Hofobi Anukfili, you know, Deep Thinker. They two and their tribes became one pair, one tribe.

And she became tribal Ogemaqkua, he tribal Ogema.

Queen and King.

Thus the Menominites had given their word of honor to return KITCH-

ITI-KI-PI, Hawatuk's anaq'ma'shena'qekan, the trinity's star-book to the tribe that thought itself the owner thereof, the Ojibwa-Chippewa.

Thus that promise was honored:

"Pehiki'wok—when two paddle The canoe on KITCH-ITI-KI-PI."

Ogema-Oshkosh, Ogemaqkua-Anaq-Mick'isik, King Bearclaw and Queen Stareye paddled the canoe of fullfilled promise.

An Ojibwa-Menomini Pictographic Myth-Legend

This nameless pictograph is copied from page 106, 14th, annual report of the Bureau of American Ethnology, the original of which was given to one Mr. J. G. Kohl by a Menomini Indian, who partly explained it to the receiver, pointing out the obvious fact, that it is—double tribal: as much Ojibwa as it is Menomini. I transcribed it into Swedish 1910, but am here developing and lenghtening that transcription, although, even now, only hinting at the meanings of the figures, of which many—yes, any could be book material.

(My original transcription of this pictograph, my Swedish, was caused by a remark, a postscript to one of my Indian articles in Svenska Dagbladet, Stockholm, Sweden.

That P. S. lifted the pictograph from the above mentioned work and page—The titanical "American Ethnology," parts thereof, can be found in all of the world's leading libraries—, lifted it, gave it as the P. S. author's own, and challenged my knowledge thus:

"*Icke ens myt—och sagobarden Baner tyder detta (Not even the Myth—and saga-bard Baner interprets this)*"

Yes, that challenge caused my original transcription.)

Kalevala-Hiawatha rhythm: Trocaic-tetra.

A—That line means: "Hear we're starting this our lay, our myth, our legend; read with care, or hearken closely—not alone to scripts and drum-sounds, but to subtler, inner meaning, hinted at, but seldom given clear deline-ations—ne'ats 1".

B—The Bear, the great Owa'ssee—brawn and brain in one, is slowly, meditatingly beginning symbolistic, mythic motions—physical—portraying mental, yes, spiritual, if transcribed by—brain and heart—sustained by fancy.

C—A wise one, yes, a teacher, giving knowledge's information to a youth that needs and wants them, both as arrows for the life bow and as strings that bind to weary feet the moqkasines of life-path.

D—The earth, with trails within it, trails upon it—thorns 'mong thistles; few and fading, withering flowers, plenty weeds, yes, poison ivies. Wisdom's shells, as yet unopened, to distribute—heart glee's pearl wines, Fragrant happi-ness and beaming—then is earth's, as well as heaven's. Yes, in due time, yes, in soon-time joy's own pearls are found by Redfolks.

E—The former pupil teaching here an other generation's aspirant for crown of learning, wisdom's laurels, knowledge's nimbus, which is here en-circling frontlet of the one that sought attainments yesterday, which he ac-quired. He, the aged one, he, the learned one soon is ready, for transmission, transmigration to Akamia, to Manidiwauk's, 2. perfected world, and tribefolk in the Bluerealm. Some one else must e'er be ready when he lifts his wings for journey toward star-world--must be ready to enshoulder knowledge's mantle: heal the tribal sores, the bodies and the hearts', the brain's, the tribe souls'. Here THIS youth is educated, like the other in his swain days, learns to heal and dry the tear-eyed. And in time he will be able to plant health-herbs where Ne'pua 3., the transformer—"Death" intended to dig graves or hammer scaffolds.

F—See, age supplanted bloom-days,—former physical—retreated, since the mental won the gloria, since it took both crown and septre there in E— when wreathing cranium. Wisdom's constellation, knowledge's star tiara, which THAT teacher gave THIS pupil, cost the former heart—and brain-toil; harsh and flaying, cost him—raven-locks. And dim-eyed he became through —mental efforts. Dim-eyed—yes . . . But—also clear-eyed. Mental senses substituted— physical, the bearish muscles—they became the wings of fancy.

G—The sign of faster humming, sign of change of canto, also; and the subject, though renewing partly that already pictured, leads the listeners, the reader—onward, subtly, but with sureness.

H—A Child is watching bird-flight: its inventive genius wakens, both the earthly one and fancy's, that which gives the 'soul-bird" pinions. Memories from many, many lives he lived, before begotten here on earth, those memories—slumbered, till he noticed wings a flutter, till he saw that bird go—wideward. "Until memories of bygone, former lives on other planets, until they are resurrected—every bantling's brain is—empty. Yes, till new experiences, those related to the former, are awakening the memories, until then—we are but—cattle" (That was said by Mianisee, Little-Owl, my deepest deep one.)

When awake, then brains are dreaming of—not only earthly comfort, but of Outworld, yes, of Skyworld—Blueworld, heaven where perfection had its homestead built by Fancy

I—Imprinting soul-won knowledge (psychclogical), a Kisha's, God's own wisdom to —the coming, next in line of tribal teachers; leaders of a generation next to his, the now developed. He, the old one, is departing for his next, perhaps the last one of his—yet unnumbered school realms. Ciceronic Kawatukan, heaven's heart-maid, soft-eyed, tender clears the path, that must be wandered by the coming tribal brain chief, heart's Ogema, of to-morrow. Kawatukan's torch-shell leads him forward, upward—Midee Wikee leads, and never did that torch flame lead into a hopeless darkness.

K—A midee priest, a doctor, with his bag of herbs, some wormwood, others sweet, but each one helpful, when prepared as effort's knowledge and experience, dripped from bygone's mystic goblet, recommended.

L—Not bird, I think, though many, among them the wise in Flambeau, so have thought; it is the symbal of a mystic, empty herb-bag. Its contents, no longer needed, is spread out 'mong lower races, than the Indians, which no longer feel the stings of gnawing sickness. It is symbolizing hope-day.

M—Division in this lore-lay.

N—Here wisdom tried, though vainly, to impart to ALL-tribes knowledge, though he knew that out of thousands—less than one gave knowledge homage.

O—A tribe-man here is walking upon road with many byroads, all bewildering, though brain-light, lighted for him by the wise ones' noble teachings, winked him forward, upward to the star-crowned hopelight, gleaming high in fancy's blue-realm, Trusts's and Hope's and—longing's region (marked by "Y",) where wreath awaits him (marked by "S"), a wreath—not wiltering.

T—Is power here, as early in this myth-lay, is Owa'ssee—yes, the bear of strength, but mental; here not leading, but—the led one.

U—The priest of Health-realm's wigwam, priest that once was tribal teacher, and with knowledge's chart and compass—led himself and youth and aged one to the realm of Glee, Akamia's. Here he tells each wanderer's legend tells wakondas and manidos—tells the spirits of—each misstep, made upon the road, but also, how the wandering ones—were trying to walk rightly, in the middle of the road that leads from Tribeworld, to where happiness has homeright.

W—The pipe—not cloudy from prophetic smoke, but beaming satisfaction's rays un-shrouded. Every question had its answer—no more reading of the mist-scripts, which that pipe did paint for tribe-wise. Every doubt and all bewildering hieroglyphic signs are clear in—west's Domain, where "Ho," is sighed to Trialworld, Tribeworld, as we named it.

X—The plate, on which the heart-maid Kawatukan serves the spirits, that were earth bound, grapes in—Blueworld, in Akamia, Redfolks' heaven.

The above gives just the first bars of this pictograph, the first canto of the lay. The rest may follow in some other of my work.

Word-Notes:

1: Ne'at, heart-friend, the foremost link in one's friend-chain. Ne'at Mita'wit is an Indian society consisting of dependable friend "whose members are MORE for each other, than for themselves." The Arapaho prophet Mianisee gave this as the origin of Ne'at Mita'wit:

"We'pot and Ne'awaq'kik, Early and Later wandered side by side over a path that was infested by rattlesnakes . . . . The day was hot, Wepot became thirsty, but had no water . . . Newaqkik had water, but no moqkasines . . . None spoke . . . Wepot bent down, unlaced one of his moqkasines, meaning to give it to the shoeless as a protection . . . stretching out his hand to deliver the shoe, his fingers touched Neawaqkik's water bag, which its owner was offering before he noticed the offer of the protecting foot-wear . . . Early and Later became so Ne'ats for life-eternity . . . ."

2: Akamia, the innermost region of Manidowauk, spirit world. "City of perfection and happiness."

3: Ne'pua, the transforming one, "death."

4: Ogema, king.

5: Midee Wikee "those holy shells, that know much, but tell, less."

6: Alltribe, the whole Indian nation.

7: Wakondas, from Wakan, super-spirit; god's sons, Manido, god.

Fallen trees and moss in bottom of Kitch-iti-ki-pi the "Big Spring". Almost mirror like reflection on account of the clearness of the water.

Waeewama's Inamaqkiu

"Waeewama's Inamaqkiu" is but one of the many links of "Ina'maqki-wok," an allegoric myth-tradition of many tribes, including Ojibway, Arapaho and Menominee. From some "old, wise ones" of the last named tribe I have learned that Menominee has a plural form of Inamaqkiu, the above given. Also that a sub clan of them exists. Inamaqki-wok means thunderbirds, and they are all special servants of either The Great One (Kisha Minido), or the Great Bad One (Matche Hawaituk). Those now remembered are: Inaq'tek, Kaka'kee, Kine'u, Shawa'nani, Pine'shiu, Opash'koshi, Pakash'tsheke'u, Pekike'kune, Ke'shewa'toche, Maq'kwo-ka'ni, Oiwat'inot, Omas'kos and Una'wanink. That is: Raven, Crow, Eagle, fork tailed Hawk, (?), a Hawk that remains as a guard-bird over winters in both Michigan and Wisconsin, sparrow Hawk (Falco Sparverius), red tailed hawk (Buteo Borealis), Beaver, (?), Squirrel.

Each of the above has a Menominee phratry named after him. And are, or were honored with a link of his own in the legendary chain "Ina'maqki'wok," Thunderbirds.

At least four or five of them "met at Kitch-iti-ki-pi on the day of the Great Spirit meeting (last of September, first of October) each year. They met on a conical hill with a flat top, near a wooded hill and a lake, located nikutwa'sata mep pa'kote'u, that is: six arrow-flights, from Kitch-iti-ki-pi. From there the thunderbirds Inaq'tek, Kaka'kee, Kine'u. Raven, Crow and Eagle, with OTHERS of their clan, followed Waban's daughters, the Morning-beams to the singing water, their own, the Moon's and the Stars' water, where each said: "Ho,ne'at, nima'nim-scaol, superfriend, I am drinking."

That reference to Kitch-iti-ki-pi makes this link of the Thunderbirds' tradition a part of the spring's own myth—and saga—chain, the work in hand.

And if we find certain old notes, we will be able to prove that "Singing Water" is—Kitch-iti-ki-pi. Those old notes will, if found, become the soul of a new myth-tradition, "Ina'maqki'wok—the thunderbirds."

Inaq'tek.

The Menominee Indian form of this myth allegory is more understandable than the symbolical versions of Arapahce, or even Nadowisiew (Sioux).

But no reader fathoms its waves by reading it as newspapers are read.

Remember that all Indian legends, myths, etc. are "double-meaning," fancy and reality combined.

Waeewama is one of Waban's many daughters. You, the white people, call our Waban "Daybreak," and his daughters are named "Morning-beams" by you.

Waeewama is the copper-tressed morning-fay, the one in linden green mantilla and pinkish moccasins, the winged kind. Matanu and Avata, Heart-

Maid and Thought Fay, are recognized, the former by her golden locks, the latter her twinkling eyes, though all three, as well as their sisters, are wing footed. So Mitanu's garments are apple green, apple bloomed, Awata's ruby striped emerald green.

Waeewama is just as love hearted as Mitanu; all Inaqteks—all ravens know that. But her temper is more fiery, her motions quicker, her tongue more sharp and—more soft. Waeewama's tresses are coppery; that and fluffed.

Waban, the father of all morning beams is the son of Keso, the Sun whose father is Hawatuk, the universal Will. So all morning beams are grand-childrens' children of Allgod.

All are behearted, bebrained, besouled.

As—everything else.

Inamaqkiu is singular AND plural of thunderbird and thunderbirds. As that clan of the bird tribe consists of Kiniu, the eagle of war, Inaqtek, the raven that understands the birch bark of myth and legend, can transform bark scripts into sounds, which he does with the tribal pawakikanaqtik, the tribal drum stick—as those two and Kakakee, the prophetic crow, all belong to the clan of thunderbirds—because of that fact we find it difficult to ascertain if Waeewama's Inamaqkiu, Morningmaid's lover, was Eagle, Raven or Crow, Kiniu, Inaqtek or Kakakee. Kakakee takes it for granted that he alone is meant. So does Kiniu. So does Inaqtek.

And only I am able to show which one is meant.

Waeewama is the queen beauty to all thunderbirds, although each loves her many sisters, adores each of them. Eagle sees a combination of courage and tenderness in her. Crow dreams her his own in the realm of realized prophecies, and Raven thinks her the personified sum total of everything adorable that has beamed since Kawatukan smiled charm creating smiles upon Allworld.

To the thunderbirds she is the incomparable.

But she is also worshipped by every tree, every bloom, every straw of grass—beloved by everything. All humanity turns east to see her and her sisters approach; all humanity turns west to see them dance into their slumber tepees.

Waeewama's lustrous locks shone morning's coppery glimmer upon and into the wigwam, wherein Inamaqkiu's cradle swung; and from her breast, from Waeewama's breast, he received the honey-colored, honey-scented milk that changed him from bantling to swain.

Virginal milk, but motherly, mothering.

The first blue seen by Inamaqkiu was that in Waeewama's tender eyes; and the first red beamed into his heart from her cheeks, her lips.

The first words he heard were "Mitan Kwitziwano" my heart-wines' goblet, and they reached him from her mouth and were sephyrically caressing.

The velvet softness of her beaming wings, the motherly, sisterly hands of a glowing sweetheart, endeared her to him from his first day in Redworld, forced him to his knees at her chariot later on.

Inamaqkiu adored Waeewama.

He worshipped her in his own dawning, at his own noontide. She became his Akamia, his heaven, when his life's afternoon arrived and in the twilight of his FIRST existence as an inamaqkiu, his first existence as a thunderbird here upon earth.

As a swain, Inamaqkiu had seen his reflection in Waeewama's and her sisters' spring, brook and lake mirrors, which had shown him to be handsome. All those reflectors had told him just that, and so had Thrush in linden-tree, Nightingale in beech. When his manhood had arrived, then the same mirrors had told him of his manliness, as did Bear and Elk.

Inamaqkiu had met Waeewama in the east, followed her to what he thought her slumber-tepee in yonder west, all during more years than many, when he, for a third time, reached mirroring waters where he expected to again stand face to face with his manhood's powerful and handsome ego. Standing at the spring and inspecting its mirage, he saw therein, not himself, but a bent, a wrinkled, a gray-locked, old man, one that he had no recollection of having noticed before.

"That," he thought so, "that ruin of a man is . . . maybe my grandfather's grandfather—his tsipai, his ghost? He worshipped not at my Waeewama's beaming altar, so resurrecting, transforming him, she did, perhaps, not re-kindle him, remake him to—to a wakonda or a manido, a demigod or a god."

All thunderbirds, Eagle, Raven and Crow—each member of that small but ruling and developing clan of the bird tribe—hate magpies, hate "ha-ha-birds." So did Waeewama's Inamaqkiu. But he could not refrain from listening to "Ha-ha, that is proud you, surely—ugly, bent and aged you—ha-ha-ha, Inamaqkiu—so called formerly."

A magpie laughed just that from the top branches of a dried, a dead spruce tree. Living, green spruces never sheltered satire's ha-ha birds; they, too, hate magpies.

On numb feet and legs, Inamaqkiu tottered toward the pool of Fancy that often had quenched desires thirst in his bygone days. But even that friend of his pictured him as gray, as wrinkled, as bent. And there too—a magpie roared its damnable: "ha-ha-ha, it's you, alright—it's YOU—the former Inamaqkiu."

For a while he thought that his eyes fooled him; he knew them to have become "a little dim—lately." For a while he thought that his ears deceived him—"they might have become a little that way." A magpie could not dare to ironize a thunderbird, he thought.

Ultimately he was forced to the conclusion that the picture in the pool and in the spring was his own image—no one else was around, so . . . And that, his conclusion, made him feel old, feel bent, feel tired. Age had over-taken him, stolen his all.

And the former swain, the former man—the aged, bent and dim-eyed and hopeless Inamaqkiu—sat down crying twixt the spring of expectation and the pool of realization.

What would his adored Waeewama think when seeing him so transformed, so bent, so wrinkled, so ugly? Just what would the ever young, ever beautiful, ever lively say—then?

Would she recognize him? And, if so, would she . . . no, she would not, could not embrace and kiss him, as she had done when he woke in his cradle, when he had become swain and man? Inamaqkiu forgot that Waeewama had done just that, that very morning at the noontide of just that day, and again before she smiled him her "goodnight" from the door of her slumber tepee in Twilight's realm.

He sighed, he cried.

He did not know that his adored one, his worshipped one, the one that had loved him through all of his earthen-life—Inamaqkiu knew not that Waeewama had noticed his gradual transformation.

And he knew not that none of Waban's of Daybreak's daughters were fickle, inconsistant, changeable, least of all his Waeewama. He did not know that Waeewama, herself, had, at least partly, dictated his transformation —she, the lifting one, the winging one; she and her sisters.

So he sighed, cried, "died."

Waeewama, Waban's copper tressed but blue-eyed charm—daughter—Inamaqkiu's goddess, did not find her lover, her worshipper on the threshold of hers, her sisters' and her father's rainbow colored wigwam in Morning's land, where her Inamaqkiu had saluted her since his feet just waddled.

The trees, shrubs, flowers—they all saluted her in their gala garb, their dew-pearled veils and cloaks. Thrush and his tribe of singing charmbirds met Waeewama at the portal twixt east and west, fancy's realm and reality's do-main. But the clan sang dirge, moaned sepulchral lutes, where it formerly touched the cymbalum's madrigalic heart-gold.

Dew-Pearls had become—tears.

Perhaps Waeewama knew why even the larks were gray-tuned—yes, she knew, she felt, because she had planned the reason for the birds' temporary sorrow.

She knew that the singers had lost—their singer—for a time.

But she sought her Inamaqkiu on her flight toward and from mittel-heaven's wigwam, where all Waban's daughters become just a glowing circle of godlike animation.

For a while.

Yes, the adored and—adoring Waeewama sought Inamaqkiu in each and all of their many trysting places twixt her father's world in far away East, her grandfather's realm in high Zenith, in near West, and ultimately in West itself, in Pashanaqkiu's domain where that lovely sister of Waeewama mixes Day's wine with Night's poppy-mead, where she brews Twilight's kwopo, the elixir of Evening's maple.

There . . . Yes on the boundary line between day and night, there, in Afterglow's vale, and Dusk's—there she found—Inamaqkiu's earthen garment. his gray wings, and . . . looking westward to where she, his queen and his goddess, Waeewama had flown a night earlier—looking westward with his sightless eyes—she found him, her Inamaqkiu's earthly ego. The spark which had moved that ego, the spark from Hichabai's forge, that she found in her own heart.

Waeewama's Inamaqkiu MUST have been INAQTEK Inamaqkiu—Dawn-beam's thunderbird MUST have been—Raven Thunderbird. Although neither Myth's bard Atanken, nor Legend's bard Atanoqken so proclaim. Kakakee Inamaqkiu, Crow Thunderbird, Kiniu Inamaqkiu, Eagle Thunderbird, the prophetic bird and the strongwinged one, they were ordered—the Crow to sing the slumberer awakening's dithyramb, the Eagle to carry that sleeper's gray wings—through west, toward east, from Slumber's valley to the glowing hilltop of Awakening.

Both Myth's bard and Legend's bard saw Waeewama's Inamaqkiu riding Eagle eastward. They heard the mystic chant of Crow. They saw Waeewama lift her wand, pronounce her incantation of—rebirth, saw her lift Inamaqkiu's soul from her own heart, smile upon it, kiss it, and—replace it in her reborn lovers heart.

And they, Legend's bard and Myth's, saw the two lovers embrace each other, kiss each other, where the blooms of anticipation become the fruit of realization—on Hope's mountain in—Faith's orient.

Who is Waeewama—have you guessed? Correct. She is the eternally beaming, all-embracing—Intuition, the blue-eyed, copper tressed, never be-clouded perceiver and distributer of glorious and ciceronic fancies. And at least two of the thunderbirds—Raven and Crow—(Bygone and future, Myth-Saga and Hope) are the earthly strings of her universal harp. The coppery tint of her locks may signify war temper (Eagle-Thunderbird); Mianisee, "The wise little owl, with whom I spent twenty interesting nights at Buckataban (Spirit Lake, Wis.) thought so. But other deep ones think that Waeewama's red and burred hair signifies rapturous exultation, the origin of skaldic such.

Inaqtik Atanoqken.

The Education of Indian Children, Religious Motivation of Their Lives

There is a general belief among white people that the native Indian children had no form of education of their own.

I have had people tell me:

"Well Mr. Baner, what you call the soul of your Indian poems and Legends, may be Indian, but no wild people can think and feel that deeply."

To convince those readers of our books that Indians can feel, think and express their thoughts and feelings, we herewith present the following article, showing that Indian children were educated, and that the Indians maintained a system which compared favorably with American methods. They were taught Dignity, Reserve, Kindness, Hospitality, Morals and Etiquette.

This is contrary to some pre-conceived notions of white people that an Indian is educated only if he has adopted the white man's concept of a high standard of living and civilization.

Dr. Gilmore, of the University of Michigan, in his manuscript on "Teaching and Training of Children As Formerly Practiced by American Indians" maintains that the Indians had an education and training which was adequate and ideal for a harmonious life under their environmental conditions.

In addition to this, Indian concepts and processes of education differed from ours, adding that in essential purpose, that of harmonious adjustment to environment, there was no great difference between the Indian's education and the white man's education.

Indians had both private and public instructions which were motivated by games, public ceremonies, story tellers, and direct special instruction. The objectives of education were personal adjustments to social customs, and training for occupations and efficient public service. Girls as well as boys were trained and taught in natural history, in religious customs, etiquette, ethics, and morals.

The disciplined and systematized form of education of the Carrier tribe on the West Coast was evidenced by the following:

Education was divided into two courses, the secular and the religious teachings. Girls were taught household duties such as preparing food, and making clothing, while boys were taught woodcraft, fishing and hunting. The secular education was usually carried on by parents and grandparents, while the religious and social education was carried on mainly by folk tale narrative.

An Indian was early impressed with the obligation of rank and responsibilities, as well as with morals and etiquete. Dignity, reserve, kindness, and hospitality were practiced extensively. Education among the Dakota nations, was similar in many respects to the Carrier tribe. Parents of these tribes were especially kind to their children, dressing them as elegantly as possible, praising and encouraging their achievements, developing in them a sense of worth, and instilling in them a family pride. Children of these tribes also participated in the social functions and organizations, and a great deal of society centered around them. Feasts were often made in honor of a boy and gifts given to him if he had accomplished some admired deed. In this manner the children were made to feel that they had honor, name, and position, to attain and maintain.

The ideals toward which the Indian was striving in the education of his children, was of course directed to develop the best mental and physical abilities, and to mould and confirm the character in the principles of dignity, honor, honesty and integrity. In a culture such as the Indians possessed, Dr. Gilmore maintains that the instrumentalities of dicipline were the most natural and efficient to carry out the Indian's ideals and to insure harmony in the environment of Indian tribal life."

W. J. Wagstaff, of Oshkosh, Wis. has the following to say in regard to the religion of the Indians: "We have seen the Indians from their oldest records as a race of people being moved on in the westward march of American aggression. We have watched them try to adjust themselves to new standards. Let us look briefly at the religious motivation of their lives."

We learn of the religious impulses of the Menominee Indians from their legends which are numerous and beautiful beyond the ability of any but a true Menominee orator to tell. Probably nothing is more typical than the teachings of the Dream Dance Lodge, a so-called pagan fraternity, still in existence. The sacred drum is the symbol of this group. It is supposed to be the symbol originally given by the great Spirit, Matcha-wah-took to an Indian woman who prayed to him with great consecration that peace might come to dwell in Indian hearts and that there might be no more warfare and that all might be brothers. There are many fetishes and ceremonies in connection with the practice of this religion, but the basic purpose is to live a good life, as taught by the cultural hero, Wa'nabus (the Indian Christ) and to receive these teachings through fasting and prayer, the revelations coming after the facts of consecration in the same way as the "Still small Voice" comes to the prayerful Christian.

Devotion to home, family, and tribe, brotherly love, self-immolation, steadfastness to obligations and allegiances, are intrinsic principles of the religion. The smoking of the sacred tobacco which carries the prayer to the Great Spirit is a holy rite as is also the beating of the sacred drum. According to the "gospel" of Wa'nabus, "When Indians come to the end of this life, they approach the river. This they must cross to get to the happy hunting grounds.

Those who have led a good life have no difficulty in crossing. They arrive at the other shore quickly. Then they hear the drums, the far-off music, and see the lights and follow them to the happy hunting grounds where they remain in eternal happiness. But those who have been bad, when they reach the river, they slip and fall and have great difficulty in reaching the other bank. When at last they do, they are confused, cannot hear the drums, cannot see the lights. They wander in trouble and darkness. But after a while they, too, begin to hear the music and see the lights and finally arrive at the happy hunting grounds. Do we believe in hell, you ask? No."

With this background, let us see the living panorama now presented to us.

A statuesque stoic bronze figure emerges from the shadows of magnificent forest, clad in buckskin. He hunts and fishes, never taking more than he needs. He rests by some spring where he drinks, a spring which he considers sacred because the earth mother so suckles her children and he is careful to protect its purity. He finds his way home to his village and his own wigwam where he is greeted affectionately by the family circle. We see the activities of the village; the groups at games, women and children and dogs; the evening village hour when the stories are told about the central fire; the night lodge fires, and then the quiet slumber. Morning brings bustle. The old men teach the children at this time, especially the smallest ones, for the young braves go with the fathers to learn the methods of the hunt, and the young maidens remain with their mothers to learn the business of homemaking.

The morning village presents a vivid picture of domestic work with its routine. This view of the stoic Indian and his life changes a little in detail; there comes the time when the village must move for the fall hunt and its replacement with the needs of the coming winter with the oval-topped wigwam of mats and skins instead of the summer wigwam of bark; the preparation of winter garments (the fur inside), the drying of meat, and then the snow-covered homes and trails, and the exigencies of the northern cold; spring brings gardening, the collecting of herbs; summer, the gathering of berries and the preparations of fish and other foods for coming winter.

We do not see these Indians on the warpath except rarely in this passing picture. They are generally occupied with getting a living and interwoven with that task is the religious devotion of a race loving the earth and the heavens by which their existence is encompassed. They are happy, jovial, imbued with piety. Inter-tribal wars sometimes come, due to misunderstandings about hunting grounds, boundaries, various aggressions or crimes, etc. But they are not entered into in haste.

The council fire is the place of long deliberation, the place for the wise words of the old men who pray and fast and "wait for the Great Spirit to speak." Warfare is their last resort, but when entered into is attended by great religious ceremony and fervor. The women become suddenly "moccasin carriers" (following the warriors with fresh moccasins and food) and guardians of the welfare of their men and papooses. Then when the carnage is over, they return to the peace they have fought for.

Into this picture, down a wide forest-edged stream comes a visitor to these shores, a French explorer, with priests and fur traders in the bateaux that make up his fleet. So the white man came to the Indians, bringing with them the puzzling problems of a different and unknown civilization.

The panorama moves quickly now over the next two or more hundred years at the end of which we see a smaller type of Indian and many, many Indians with lighter skins, who wear some of the white man's trappings, ape some of his ways including his vices, and on a whole are a disorganized, wavering, confused group of humans holding on, to the shreds of their former greatness.

Ona'way-Ok'sha.

CPSIA information can be obtained
at www.ICGtesting.com
Printed in the USA
BVOW09s2000061117

62BV00028B/1475/P